Complex Histories, Contested Memories
Some Reflections on Remembering Difficult Pasts

THE DOREEN B. TOWNSEND CENTER FOR THE HUMANITIES was established at the University of California at Berkeley in 1987 in order to promote interdisciplinary studies in the humanities. Endowed by Doreen B. Townsend, the Center awards fellowships to advanced graduate students and untenured faculty on the Berkeley campus, and supports interdisciplinary working groups, lectures, and team-taught graduate seminars. It also sponsors symposia and conferences which strengthen research and teaching in the humanities, arts, and related social science fields. The Center is directed by Candace Slater, Professor of Spanish and Portuguese. Christina M. Gillis has been Associate Director of the Townsend Center since 1988.

————————————————— ■ —————————————————

COMPLEX HISTORIES, CONTESTED MEMORIES: SOME REFLECTIONS ON REMEMBERING DIFFICULT PASTS is the text of a lecture Eva Hoffman gave while visiting the Townsend Center as Una's Lecturer in the Humanities for Fall 2000. In addition to the lecture, Hoffman read from her recent work, and participated in a follow-up discussion with faculty from UC Berkeley and other universities. Paul Alpers, who was the Townsend Center's founding director, introduces this volume. Una's Lectures in the Humanities, endowed in the memory of Una Smith Ross, Berkeley class of 1911, are administered by the Townsend Center for the Humanities.

————————————————— ■ —————————————————

Funding for the OCCASIONAL PAPERS of the Doreen B. Townsend Center for the Humanities is provided by the Dean of the Graduate Division, and by other donors. Begun in 1994-95, the series makes available in print and on-line some of the many lectures delivered in Townsend Center programs. The series is registered with the Library of Congress. For more information on the publication, please contact the Doreen B. Townsend Center for the Humanities, 220 Stephens Hall, The University of California, Berkeley, CA 94720-2340, http://ls.berkeley.edu/dept/townsend, (510) 643-9670.

————————————————— ■ —————————————————

Occasional Papers Series
Editor: Christina M. Gillis
Assistant Editor & Production: Jill Stauffer
Printed by Hunza Graphics, Berkeley, California

ISBN   1-881865-23-1
Occasional Papers of the Doreen B. Townsend Center for the Humanities, no. 23.

Contents

Preface

It is a great pleasure for me to introduce Eva Hoffman as Una's Lecturer for the year 2000. Una's Lectures were established to commemorate a remarkable woman who came to Berkeley from South Dakota, early in the 20th century, and discovered her intellectual and moral powers as a student here. In endowing Una's Gift, her husband, Edward Hunter Ross, associated her intellectual restlessness, vigor and independence with the characteristics of the university itself, "remote from Eastern centers of learning." Berkeley is rather less remote from the east coast universities than it was a century ago, and is no longer, as Hunter Ross's words imply, in their shadow. But those of us who teach here still find ourselves encountering remarkable students from all kinds of places and walks of life, and it is encouraging to feel, as we enter a new century, this connection between Una Smith's Berkeley and our own.

Many distinguished scholars and writers have served as Una's Lecturer, but none is more fitting than Eva Hoffman. As you know from her memoir, *Lost in Translation*, her own intellectual vigor and independence emerged in and were shaped by a distinctive life's journey. It began in Poland, where she was born at the very end of World War II, and led her to the west coast of North America—where, as an adolescent in Vancouver, she found considerably less spiritual fulfillment than did Una Smith in Berkeley—and to the eastern centers of learning: Yale, where she did graduate work in music, and Harvard, where she earned a Ph.D. in English and

American literature. The talents so evident in *Lost in Translation* led her not to the academic world, but to the world of serious journalism. For more than ten years, she was an editor and book critic at *The New York Times*, and I imagine that her three years as senior editor of its "Book Review" had a good deal to do with its emergence from mediocrity.

But it is in her books that one most fully discovers Eva Hoffman's intelligence and distinction. *Lost in Translation* is already something of a classic; at a time when there is a bewildering proliferation of choices of what to read, it is one of the books that almost everyone you meet seems to have read and admired. Her most recent book, *Shtetl*, won the Bronislaw Malinowski Social Science Award from the Polish Institute of Arts and Sciences. In lucid, thoughtful prose, it combines a concrete account of one Polish village and its people with a view of the entire historical sweep of the history of the Jews in Poland. It has particularly drawn attention, as we continue to experience the aftermaths of the Holocaust, for its humane polemic against ethnic stereotyping. Between the human richness and ironic poise of *Lost in Translation* and the historical intelligence and ambition of *Shtetl*, Eva Hoffman's second book, *Exit into History*, may be in danger of fading into the background. I hope this will not be the case. The book recounts her meetings with citizens, mostly professionals and intellectuals, in four countries of Eastern Europe after the fall of the Communist regimes. Page after page testifies to her ability to listen, observe, and assess the difficult lives her friends and new acquaintances have lived and the lives they find themselves entering into. No one can speak with more engagement and understanding about such difficult lives. Indeed, such lives are the subject of her lecture tonight.

—Paul Alpers
Professor of English, Emeritus, UC Berkeley

Complex Histories, Contested Memories
Some Reflections on Remembering Difficult Pasts

Eva Hoffman

I want to reflect on two related matters: First, the current preoccupation with memory, and its possible sources; and second, the way that memory has exercised itself on a particularly complex and highly contested history—the history of Polish Jews, and of Polish-Jewish relations.

The first subject is so elusive and protean that I can only hope it won't slip through my fingers as I speak. Memory, of course, has become one of the master terms of current intellectual discourse, and to some extent, of popular discourse as well. The preoccupation with memory seems to be general all over America. After a wave of interest in individual forms of memory and its distortions—false memory, recovered memory, post-traumatic memory—we have entered a phase of fascination with collective or group memory, which is nearly always equated with remembrance of traumatic historical events. The Nanking massacre for the Chinese Americans, the great famine for the Irish Americans—these become the defining episodes whose "memory" is called upon as a guarantee of group identity and, often, its moral status. And, as has been often noted, the Holocaust, for evident reasons, has become the paradigm of traumatic collective memory—indeed, the model for current thinking about memory altogether.

I must confess that I have often been baffled by the ubiquitousness of memory talk, by the sheer emphasis on this most slippery and elusive of human faculties. We all know the vagaries, the changeability, the frequent unreliability of personal memory: the way that whole episodes or segments of the past can be forgotten or foregrounded at different times of our lives, depending on our present state, aims and self-definition. When it comes to collective or group memory, things become even more problematic. Whose memories, really, are we talking about? How are they known, how do they come to us? In other words, to what extent are collective memories memories at all, rather than received ideas or historical fables? Sometimes, perhaps as with any term that is too frequently used, one begins to suspect that when we so casually, or so reverently, allude to "memory," we are merely making a gesture in the direction of something that has come to have vaguely lyrical, or vaguely significant, or even vaguely transcendent association.

And yet, of course, we cannot do without some conception of memory, as we cannot do without memory itself. For all its protean malleability, memory is crucial to our sense of a continuous self; and on the collective level, too, we need some shared sense of the past in order to feel ourselves members of the same group, or tribe, or—*pace* Margaret Thatcher, who thought there was no such thing—society.

How, then, shall we think about memory? And what is the relationship of group memories to the "real past," so to speak—to the histories from which they supposedly emerge and to which they supposedly refer?

The proper relationship of memory to history has been extensively debated in recent years, but that relationship varies vastly in different circumstances and situations. For example, as anyone growing up in Eastern Europe after the Second World War was aware, in the Soviet Union and the countries under its Communist dispensation, memory was the only guarantee of a truthful history. When official history writing offered deliberate and ruthless lies, when it deleted horrific events and entire groups and nationalities from the historical record, people literally had to rely on private, local, subversive memory to preserve the true version—the fundamental facts, even—of what happened. Hence, the passionate defense of local knowledge and of fidelity to the past by Eastern European writers such as Czeslaw Milosz and Milan Kundera.

Joseph Yerushalmi, in his seminal book *Zakhor*, has written of a very different relationship between memory and history, a relationship in which a religiously sanctioned memory has powerful moral primacy, and historical consciousness is either absent or thought of as unnecessary. Throughout much Diasporic history, Yerushalmi argues, the meaning and the destiny of the Jewish people were envisioned as a cyclical reiteration of foundational events, and interpreted through this archetypal prism. The expulsion from Spain, for example, was seen as a repetition of the expulsion from Egypt; the massacres during the Crusades as a new instance of the persecutions in Roman times. In this vision of eternal recurrence, events taking place in the present or near past were incorporated into the ancient narratives and encoded into collective memory through ritual remembrance.

One can observe yet other shuttlings and transactions between the terms "memory" and "history": for example, a relationship in which private and tribal memory is recruited in the service of official aims, and becomes the realm of deliberate distortion and falsification—as happened in the recent wars in former Yugoslavia. And there are surely situations in which the relationship between history and memory is more reciprocal and responsible, and history writing becomes an active element in the formation of a group's or a nation's memory.

By comparison, the current conversation about memory seems oddly deflected and oblique. The fascination with this term, and faculty, seems not to exist within any framework of belief, nor to have any distinct aims. If we take the Holocaust as a paradigm for this preoccupation, then it can be said that memory has been used in the service of mourning. But the often reiterated invocations to remember, the building of commemorative Holocaust museums in provincial American towns, the focus on the aesthetics of commemoration, the often lyricized analyses of the processes of traumatic remembering or its witnessing—these seem not so much to mourn past events, as to foreground memory itself as something of value, an almost spiritual faculty, or a kind of late post-modern moral good.

There have been many reasons suggested for the current ascendancy of memory discourse in America: the trauma of the Vietnam war leading to an interest in post-traumatic syndromes, which are often characterized either by the suppression or by a nightmarish fixity of recollection; the rise of identity politics, with its privileging of particular pasts as opposed to a totalizing, melting-pot kind of historical account; and finally, the deliberate politicization of certain historical events—especially the Holocaust—and their exploitation and reification for ideological uses, such as Zionism.

I think all these explanations have merit and describe real phenomena. But I want to add another element which I think affects the atmosphere and the tone of our particular preoccupation with memory, and that is the element of distance—both temporal and spatial distance—at which we stand vis à vis the past which preoccupies us. What I want to suggest is that the current wave of memory discourse is partly a generational phenomenon; that it has emerged from what could loosely be called the "post" generation—that is, the generation that comes immediately after the event; and that moreover, in America, the spatial and cultural remoteness from the histories that we want to "remember" also affects the character of our relationship to the past.

In focusing on its generational aspects, I want to take the psychological roots of the memory phenomenon seriously; but I want to bring some critical skepticism to its results. Again, if we take the Holocaust to be the originating paradigm for the broader exploration of memory, then we can see that the intensive interest in the problematic of memory (as opposed to questions of history or experience) has emerged late, and has been impelled not by the participants in the events but by those who stand at a kind of proximate remove from them. The participants in the events usually don't thematize memory in the same way—perhaps because they have so much to remember. The memoirs written by Holocaust survivors rarely pause to reflect on the processes of memory; rather, they tend to follow straightforward mimetic conventions, in which a realistic account is taken to correspond to the events as they took place. In other words, memory in these texts usually is taken for granted.

The intense preoccupation with memory itself, as opposed to its referents, has largely emerged from the generation "after"—a generation to which I belong, and which is now reaching (alas!) its later middle age, the age of all kinds of returns and researches into the past. For that generation—for my generation—the Second World War, with its central trauma of the Holocaust, has been a crucially formative event. It has loomed over our collective consciousness; it has to a large extent formed that consciousness. And yet, it is an event which we did not experience ourselves.

What does it mean to stand in that kind of relationship to a significant, indeed a formative past? Here I am going to allow myself to speak personally for a few moments, since the phenomena I want to talk about are quite interior, and have to do, more than anything else, with a certain formation of subjectivity. That formation can perhaps be seen most vividly among the literal "second generation" to which I happen to belong; both my parents endured and survived the cataclysm of the Holocaust within Poland, and I myself grew up in Poland after the war. But while I'm going to make some autobiographical remarks, I hope I'm not being merely personal. The kinds of second-generation experiences I want to mention have been extensively studied and written about, both by children of survivors and others; and by now we know that certain patterns of response and feeling are widely shared.

For the children of survivors—and indeed, children of all participants in the war— the knowledge of that forbidding event was transmitted in very intimate ways. It was passed on through private stories, through family speech, or indeed family silences. That speech —this recurs again and again in the literature on the subject—was often incoherent, fragmented, broken; it came in encapsulated, explosive phrases; it was speech under the pressure of great pain. It took me a long time to put together a chronological sequence from the fragments and phrases; and I know that others have found it equally difficult. When I was a child, these capsules, or eruptions, of narrative suggested an utterly irrational world, in which final, absolute things happened without cause or effect. Most terrible acts struck from a vacuum; there was no point in inquiring for reasons. Horrifying and irrational as the actual events were, they seemed, in my childhood mind, more horrifying and irrational still.

But, aside from their enormity, the memories of the Holocaust, and of the war, had another quality—that of enormousness. The moments remembered by survivors were usually those of utmost tension or danger, moments in which life and death hung in the balance; the very extremity of the compressed phrases conveyed a drama which in a sense was superhuman.

Since I grew up in Poland, almost everyone, Jewish and non-Jeiwsh, had their chronicles of suffering and loss: of relatives who had been murdered, or sent to Siberia, or imprisoned after the war—with a horrible irony—for resisting the Nazis. There were also images of cities reduced to rubble, of crumbling buildings and gaping windows.

These images were close enough and haunting enough to seem almost mine. But even though they became deeply imprinted on my mind, I don't think I ever made the mistake of thinking they were mine. Instead, like so many second-generation children, I felt I was their designated carrier; they were entrusted to me. But that meant—perhaps even more than for my parents—that I couldn't really question, or interpret, or even think about the awful past. I could only repeat what had been told to me, honor it by exact retelling. There was a deeply internalized duty not to let diffusion, or revision, or forgetfulness, take its course. And there was also the need to respect the silences, the lacunae, the privacy of grief. This meant that there was also an element of prohibition on coherence. To make a sequential narrative of "what happened then" would have been to make indecently rational what was obscenely irrational. It would have been to normalize through form an utterly aberrant content.

But, in addition to these empathetic and awed responses, there were perhaps more dubious, or at least less selfless reasons for the fixed preservation of memories—and for my identification with them. There was a kind of fear of demystification. In a sense, I wanted to keep these parental experiences enormous, in both senses of the word. And perhaps, as in all identification, there was an element of envy as well as compassion. My parents, and others like them, had lived through something ultimate; my own experiences would always be trivial by comparison.

Even for those who did not grow up in its immediate proximity, the war is a powerful legacy in our generation. We grew up on literature and imagery of ultimate danger and ultimate choices, on landscapes of ruin and desolation. Many of us heard stories of that time from parents or relatives, or others who had lived through it. Even if we didn't, we became gradually aware that enormous and tragic events took place in the preceding generation, events which we did not experience ourselves, but which were close enough to us in time to seem almost a part of our own, so to speak, prehistory—close enough to constitute transmitted memories. And I wonder whether our foregrounding of memory (as opposed to understanding, say, or experience, or, indeed, history) is in part a mid-life return to our own early memories—our memories of powerful, transmitted memories; I wonder if there is in this preoccupation an attempt to make sense of the shadowy stories and potent images that we first received as fragmentary, frightening, fascinating knowledge—received differently, that is, from those who had lived through the events themselves, or even witnessed them as adults. Indeed, to make a risky suggestion, it seems to me that in the strange obliqueness and ambiguity of our current memory-discourse, one can discern a kind of transposition of childhood modalities of perception into the formulations of adult theory and thought. One can note this transposition in the concern with keeping the enormity of catastrophic events pure; in the almost religious awe that we bring to stories of survivors; in the frequent insistence on keeping memory itself in a kind of mystical state, with the gaps, the fragmentation, the profound unknowability intact. In other words, I think there has been a kind of transmutation of child-hood awe into a rhetoric of sacralization—of the unimaginable, the unspeakable, the untouchable: a conception of horrific events as something that has to be remembered in its fixed state, even if it cannot be known.

Of course, all of this is understandable and to some extent legitimate, and in a sense this is something that happens in every generation. When we are grow-ing up, our parents, or the parental generation, stand for the Real, for how the human world is put together and how we know it. And the events that constitute our parental legacy have a kind of overwhelming reality. They were awful, and command awe. They also command compassion and fidelity. The suffering of those who endured the events needs to be acknowledged, commemorated, mourned. And yet, a fixed piety towards this history does not seem to me sufficient to the occasion; the attempt to identify with the older generation's experience—the insistence that we can identify with it through memory—can verge on a kind of appropriation, or even bad faith. The experience was emphatically not ours, and in our desire to merge with it, to bridge the distance through a sheer claim of memory rights, one can perhaps detect a sort of envy, a fascination with the elemental drama that the previous generation has lived through with a knowledge garnered from extremity. The pasts we attempt to "remember" were terrible, but they had *terribilitas* and a dark grandeur.

Perhaps our fascination with tragic legacies—our idealization of cata-strophe—derives in part from the sense that in our "post-" generation, we have had too many experiences and not enough profound experience, too much information and not enough history. Memory is the faculty through which we can claim to connect with a significant past, or maybe even with the sense of significance itself—for the very word memory has begun to be used as a sort of stand-in for the authentic or the real, especially, of course, for the authenticity and the reality of suffering. The vicarious urge to partake of, to "participate" in such authenticity is evident, for example, in the widespread "tragedy tourism": visits to former slave quarters in Africa, or mass tours of concentration camps.

In a way, it seems to me that in the turn to memory we are doing the opposite of what Freud called disavowal—that we are practicing a kind of avowal. Disavowal is the strategy whereby we deny, or sometimes literally do not see, something that may be right in front of us, but that is too disturbing to acknowledge. In our strategy of avowal, we declare that we remember, identify with, defend, something extremely disturbing that we have not experienced—and that we simultaneously declare to be unimaginable. We avow, or vow ourselves, to be faithful to a past that, in a way, we refuse to know.

But the question is: What should we, in the second generation, do with the received, transferred memories? Do we have the right to touch upon them, so to speak, to dis-identify from them, to examine them from different viewpoints, or insert them into a coherent narrative or structure of interpretation? My answer is that not only do we have the right, we have the obligation to do so. I think that is exactly our task in the second generation: not only to honor and remember but to think about the past strenuously and to investigate memory rigorously.

That doesn't mean it is easy to do. In psychoanalytic thought—and in our time, it is psychoanalysis which has provided the richest account of memory and its workings—it is recognized that separating the past from the present is a considerable psychic accomplishment. Indeed, it can be said that the aim of memory-work in psychoanalysis is to establish the sense of the past, to understand the past consciously so that we do not have to struggle unconsciously under its dictates. On a broader scale, this is something that every generation has to do: understand its heritage in its own way and separate itself from it sufficiently so that it does not have to repeat it, or even invert it, inversion being often a camouflaged form of repetition.

When the generational inheritance includes tragedy, the task becomes more difficult. Both the fear of violating a legacy of great suffering and the force of prohibition on rethinking and revising the formulae of memory are powerful. And yet, I think that if we do not do this—if we do not make the next move—we will end up being truly unfaithful to the legacy we are ostensibly honoring and preserving: unfaithful to its reality and complexity, and to the possibility of understanding. Surely if we are to understand the legacy of the Holocaust, and other disturbing pasts, we must stand in an investigative relationship to memory; we must acknowledge our distance—both generational and cultural—from the events which we're trying to comprehend. But it seems to me that if we are to deepen our comprehension, we need also to use that distance to try to see aspects of the past that may not have been perceptible at other moments and from other perspectives.

In my case, the field of address for these issues has been the history of Polish Jews and Polish-Jewish relations. On one level, in turning to this subject, I was examining my own and my family's extended history—that is, I was beginning with intimate memory, and trying to understand it via history. My parents had both grown up in a shtetl very much like the one I wrote about in my book *Shtetl*—a town in the part of the Ukraine which was Polish before the war and reverted to Soviet hands after it. They survived the war, against all statistical odds, in their own village, with the help of Poles and Ukrainians who were risking their own lives in order to save my parents. At the same time, my parents felt the threat of informing and violence from some parts of the local population. These were the memories which I had taken in, internalized, since childhood; now I wanted to place them within a longer and a broader context.

But I thought there were other reasons to write about Polish-Jewish history. One was simply that it is a very rich and intriguing history, which has remained, especially in America, virtually unknown. In terms of American-Jewish self-understanding specifically, it is a very salient, indeed a central past, but is also a history which is often understood through the most reductive, received formulae, and which seems to be surrounded almost by a taboo on rethinking.

At the same time, the history of the Polish-Jewish relationship is one of the most complex examples of a contested past—of which we have so many other unhappy instances. We can see the horrific consequences of stuck, conflicting memories in such places as Ireland or Yugoslavia, or, for that matter, the Middle East. In a sense, the Polish past, particularly during the Holocaust, is more debatable than German history during the same period. In the case of Nazism, the moral rights and wrongs were starkly clear, and, broadly speaking, both Germans and Jews today take the same view of what happened. But the Polish-Jewish past is the embattled terrain of several collective memories, each with its claim to moral legitimacy, and each charged with fierce and sometimes vehement feelings.

In Jewish memory, Poland holds an exceptional place, for that is largely where the Holocaust was executed. Most of the concentration camps were situated in Nazi-occupied Poland, and in many people's minds, by a kind of elision, this implies that the Holocaust was a Polish event, or that the Nazis decided to place concentration camps there because they counted on the cooperation of the natives. This has been repeatedly shown to be entirely untrue. It is much more likely that the camps were placed in occupied Polish territory because that was where the majority of the Jewish population slated for extermination lived. The behavior of individual Poles during that period differed widely, and ranged, as in many other countries, from hostile and sometimes violent acts against Jews, to courageous and sometimes self-sacrificing efforts at rescue. But our minds are associative: because the destruction took place there, because such enormous losses were incurred, Poland has come to figure in Jewish consciousness as the very heart of darkness, as contaminated ground.

In Polish memory, the war is the time of Polish tragedy. About three million non-Jewish Poles died in the war, as well as three million Jewish ones. In Nazi ideology, Poles were designated an inferior race, and were slated, if not for wholesale extermination, then for enslavement. Auschwitz, as Poles will often point out, was initially built for Polish prisoners, and, although all the figures in this unhappy area are being revised, it was thought until recently that over 300,000 Poles died there. The Polish resistance movement against the Nazis was the largest and most socially encompassing of any European country. Aside from the Warsaw Ghetto Uprising, there was also the now less well remembered Warsaw uprising, in which 250,000 people died and Warsaw was reduced to rubble within a few weeks. While the uprising was taking place, the supposedly friendly Soviet army was waiting on the other side of the Vistula River, waiting for the German army to destroy the city; when it was over, the Soviets walked in to occupy it.

The extreme bitterness of these events could never be properly processed within Poland itself because of the subsequent clamp-downs of censorship, and the blatant falsifications of Communist historiography. The Holocaust, and Polish behavior vis à vis the most threatened part of the country's population, became one of the forbidden subjects—what the Poles later came to call "the blank stains" within collective, or at least public, memory. So, incidentally, did the role of the Polish non-Communist resistance, whose members were hardly thanked after the war for what they had done. Indeed, they were widely persecuted by the Communist regime, sentenced to long terms in prison, and in some cases, executed. Still, on the Jewish side, the seeming forgetfulness by their Polish neighbors of the annihilating catastrophe added enormously to the sense of rancor and grievance.

The Cold War also shaped collective memories of the West, particularly the American and Jewish-American comprehension of these faraway events. For the decades of the Cold War, Eastern Europe was cut off from living contact with the West. Moreover, in the American imagination, Poland, like other countries in the region, was perceived as the totalitarian, evil empire—the new arch-enemy. I think that those images attached themselves to earlier conceptions of Eastern Europe as a savage or primitive realm, and became reified, or petrified, into a kind of mythology that seemed to be in no need of examination or revision. And so, while the American, and, indeed, Jewish-American conceptions of Germany underwent considerable processing and revision, and while it was increasingly understood that Nazism had to be distinguished from Germanness, no such differentiations or discriminations were deemed necessary in the Polish case. It remained quite possible to speak of Polish anti-Semitism as if it were an essential quality of the national character, or to say that Poles drank anti-Semitism with their mother's milk, etc. This, in turn, increased Poles' bitterness at the exaggerations of their country's wrongdoing during the war, and the world's indifference to its wartime suffering.

It seemed to me, as I set out to write *Shtetl*, that in order to understand each of these tribal, collective memories—and the fissures between them—I had to bring them into dynamic interaction, as they actually were during their long coexistence. In other words, this was a case in which none of the memories could be understood in isolation, or simply on its own terms by a kind of avowal of loyalty.

The other problem in thinking about Polish-Jewish history—and another reason why it offers such an important template for current questions of memory—is that it presents such a powerful example of a memory which has undergone a kind of traumatic fixation. The understanding of Polish-Jewish history, especially in the Western Jewish imagination, has been frozen at the point of cataclysm. On the popular level, almost everything else about it has been forgotten, or reduced to mythopoeic images. And so, my other aim was to try to unfreeze the understanding in this area—to get beyond the points of the formulaic images, but also of trauma. It seemed to me that it was necessary to do so even if one wanted to deepen one's understanding of what happened during the Holocaust itself.

Fortunately, the history itself is fascinating, and, as one of the longest examples of cross-ethnic and cross-religious coexistence, relevant not only for Jewish self-understanding, but to our broader contemporary situation. After all, Jews had lived in Poland for over eight centuries. For several of those centuries, Poland had the largest Jewish population of any country in the world in absolute numbers, and the largest percentage by far of Jewish people. While the Jewish population in Germany had always hovered under the two percent mark, the Jewish minority in Poland, from the eighteenth century on, constituted between ten and thirteen percent of the total population. There were three and half million Jews in Poland before the war. Warsaw—just to animate these figures for you—was forty percent Jewish in the interwar period. Throughout many centuries, Jews were a significant, highly visible and not entirely powerless minority. In effect the Polish-Jewish coexistence was a kind of extended experiment in multiculturalism *avant la lettre*. So, the history is pertinent to us; but at the same time, in writing about it, I found it very helpful to bring to it observations garnered from American, and increasingly Western European, experience. Until World War II, Eastern Europe was the melting pot of Europe; and in the light of our own, more recent experience of multiculturalism, we can better appreciate and analyze the problems and tensions of these earlier heterogeneous societies. In the light of that experience, I believe that some of the conflicts in Polish-Jewish history can be seen in terms of majority-minority tensions, rather than in terms of strong and specific anti-Semitism.

At the same time, Polish-Jewish history offers a varied and suggestive template for the study of unexpected and unfamiliar forms of and propositions for multicultural coexistence. For example, I was fascinated to read the Statute of Kalisz, which was the first piece of legislation regulating the affairs of the Jewish minority in Poland. Written in 1263, this document extended far-reaching protections and privileges to the Jewish community, including complete legal and religious autonomy. Moreover, the Statute tried to forestall and restrain anti-Semitic prejudices common at the time. For example, it forbid the accusation of "ritual libel" which often led to anti-Jewish violence in Medieval Europe, and specified that a Christian who makes such an accusation falsely would suffer the same punishment as the Jewish person would have, had the accusation been true. In other words, this Medieval document surprises by its advocacy of tolerance, and its far-reaching attempt to address the concerns of a group that was likely to meet with intolerance.

Later periods witness the creation of fascinating institutions such as the Council of Four Lands, which functioned from the mid-sixteenth until the mid-eighteenth century and was in effect a kind of parliament, or a governing body of a highly independent, and by that time large, minority. The Council consisted of elected representatives from the numerous Jewish communities; it met four times a year to discuss and legislate the affairs of the Jewish "nation," as it had come by then to be called. The council collected taxes, sent lobbyists to the Polish parliament, and tried to promote laws and regulations advantageous for the Jewish constituency.

Indeed, one reason to study the longer history of Polish Jews is to remember that Jews were neither passive nor unimplicated in their own history. As Joseph Yerushalmi reminds us, Jewish history has often been viewed as taking place within cycles of eternal recurrence, and in an essentially ahistorical framework—and this tendency has its own consequences. Certainly, the Eastern European shtetl lived largely under the aegis of religious laws, and remained largely static throughout its existence. But at the same time, the Jewish inhabitants of Poland—the rabbinical leadership among them—were aware of their community's actual, historical situation and tried to work on behalf of its interests. They tried to influence the Polish ruling powers; they decided which policies they wanted to support or not; they administered the affairs of the Jewish "nation" as a whole, and negotiated its disputes.

In an eye-opening book, *Power and Powerlessness in Jewish History*, the historian David Biale gives an account of Jewish political life in the Diaspora, and shows that through the long centuries of exile, Jews used conscious political theories and political institutions to negotiate their own affairs and relationship with the governing powers of the countries in which they found themselves. Biale's account is not so much in argument with Yerushalmi's thesis as an important supplement to it. The interests of Diasporic Jews ran mainly to the preservation of a traditional, religious, separate identity; so politics was used, one could say, in the service of destiny—in the service of maintaining that ahistorical vision of their fate that Yerushalmi describes.

In this fundamental aim, the Jews of Poland to a large extent succeeded, though it was success that carried its own price. However, the shtetl, judged by these criteria, was a remarkably resilient social formation, preserving its structures and its religious, legal and educational autonomy over centuries. In the Jewish imagination, the shtetl has become the locus of nostalgia and the metaphor of loss; it is usually seen as a quaint realm, either of Chagall-like innocent spirituality, or of Cossacks and pogroms. But one of the features of the shtetl which struck me was its high level of organization. Symbolically, life was structured by a system of religious belief that governed every aspect of behavior, from eating, to sexuality, to the shaping of the day, the week, the year. More concretely, the shtetl was organized into a network of brotherhoods, societies, and associations, ranging from the important burial brotherhoods to societies for the aid of poor finances and later, cooperative banking associations.

It is quite possible that these communal organizations were a precursor and a preparation for the amazing explosion of Jewish political life which took place in Poland in the interwar period. This interval of Polish independence saw both the rise of ideological, nationalist anti-Semitism, and an exfoliation of Jewish life and creativity, which included the formation of many political parties, the election of numerous Jewish representatives to the Polish parliament, and ongoing, heated debates about the proper relationship between the Jewish minority and the Polish majority.

I do not mean to offer a highlights tour of Polish-Jewish history, but only to suggest—admittedly in severely curtailed shorthand—that the history had many phases, and that it was not only a narrative of Jewish victimhood and Polish oppression. However, one of the fervently debated questions in the field of Polish-Jewish relations is whether there was any continuity between pre-Holocaust Polish history and attitudes, and Polish behavior during the Holocaust itself. The nature of that behavior is also the subject of painful disputes.

The behavior in fact covered the entire spectrum of human possibilities—much as it did in other countries. In the shtetl which I studied, I was told of the kinds of episodes which were reenacted in countless localities throughout Poland. There were Poles who helped rescue Jews, sometimes on an impulse, and sometimes with the full knowledge that they were endangering their own and their families' lives; there were those who informed on their Jewish neighbors, or colluded more actively in anti-Jewish violence, with a variety of motives: for payment, for petty revenge, or out of sheer anti-Semitism. There was a story I was told by a survivor whose entire family was killed in one moment by the local Gestapo, who had probably been notified of their whereabouts by a Polish passer-by. He and another man were kept alive by a family of Polish peasants who built a special hiding place for them, and took enormous and conscious risks over a period of nearly two years to aid them. I think it needs to be remembered that in the awful calculus of the time, it took one act of meanness to end the lives of many; it took the efforts of many to save one Jewish life.

Still, the question of continuity between Polish history and Polish behavior during the Holocaust—that is, the question of intrinsic Polish anti-Semitism—is one on which the views of the various participants most painfully diverge. The Polish participants remind us that Poland was the only country that experienced two invasions—one from Germany, and the other from the Soviet Union. They would say—they have said—that the Jewish populations of the eastern shtetls actively welcomed the Soviets, who were Poland's historical enemy and occupiers. The Jewish inheritors of this history reiterate that it made sense for Jews to welcome the Soviets, who were seen by them as a much lesser evil than the Nazis, and who brought with them the promises of universal equality and the erasure of ethnic and class differences. Once the Nazi occupation went into full effect, it created unprecedented conditions, which were perhaps more horrifying than anywhere in Europe. In terms of attitudes towards Jews, the situation imposed by the Nazi occupation was one of grotesquely warped morality. Within the Nazi universe, helping and rescuing Jews was punishable by death, whereas giving one's Jewish neighbors away was rewarded—albeit very poorly. Within this perverted framework, there were people who behaved odiously, and people who behaved heroically; and there was the great majority which was indifferent or indeed ignorant of the tragedy happening in its midst. In their own terms, both parties are right. How can one, then, evaluate—never mind reconcile—their claims, the claims of still living, still rankling memories?

Or, to put this question differently: Can one, in interpreting this extremely difficult past, move beyond the point of view of its participants? Can one, in particular, step away from the perspective of the most victimized subjects? Until now, it has seemed indecent to do so. In our thinking about memory, the perspective of the victims has been the touchstone—and this to some extent has remained untouchable; it has seemed beyond interrogation. And I believe that on the individual level, it should be. The testimony of personal suffering—especially of the degree endured during the Holocaust—should not and cannot be questioned "objectively." It can, at best, be listened to and understood. And, on the individual level, acts of violence or cruelty against the victims can only be condemned.

But on the collective level, in situations and histories as complex and contested as the Polish one, I think one has to gain a more holistic, more contextual understanding: to understand the interaction of various participants, and the structure of the situation as a whole. Otherwise, one runs the risk of only repeating the separate narratives, and replicating the lack of understanding between them. The historian Saul Friedlander in his book, *Memory, History and the Extermination of the Jews*, speaks of the impossibility of thinking about the Holocaust outside one's own subject position. Nor do I think for a moment that I could step outside my own subject position—outside my actual experience and family memories, in other words—or that it is desirable for anyone to do so. I think that, in any case, there is hardly such a thing as impartial thinking; unless we are writing from a very long temporal or affective distance, we almost necessarily begin from a mental location, so to speak, and a point of view. On the other hand, there is no contradiction between point of view and strenuous thought. And I think that if one presses one's own subject position far enough, one eventually always encounters the Other. For no history, and certainly no Jewish history, has taken place in isolation. Now, encountering the Other cannot always lead to reconciliation. There are situations in which the injustices committed in the past, or the inequities of power, are so extreme, that a structural understanding can lead only to an acknowledgment of the wrongs of the past. Of course, if such acknowledgment is made by both sides, that can be helpful and can even aid in healing. But in histories as entangled as the Polish-Jewish one—histories which resemble more closely the tangled politics of our own societies—to think of any one group's memory without taking the other into account is to deny the real conditions of that group's existence. And I think that if one does examine any one subject position far enough, one also comes upon one's own weaknesses, or prejudices and projections towards the other—for no one, not even minority groups, are without them.

Since the history of Polish-Jewish relations is so long and varied, it offers a very large field within which one can start asking certain basic questions. One underlying question which concerned me as I was thinking about this past is: what makes for harmonious cross-cultural relations, and what makes them break down? Certainly, the elements of religious and later ideological anti-Semitism in the majority culture affected the relationship between Poles and Jews greatly. And yet, despite this, there were decades and even centuries in their common history when the two groups lived side by side amicably, or at least in a state of benign indifference. This is something that I think needs to be taken into account. We tend to parse the past through its climactic moments—that is, the moments of violence and conflict. But the long phases in which nothing very notable happened between Poles and Jews suggest to me that the instinct of tolerance is as basic as its opposite, and that when hostilities are not actively stimulated, people and groups are capable of accepting each other, for all their cultural and spiritual differences. The eruptions of active hostility within Polish society usually took place during periods of heightened economic competitiveness, or marked conflict of interest—and there were times, as during various Russian occupations of Poland, when actual Polish and Jewish political interests diverged to a considerable degree.

Still, the deepest and the most obvious factor affecting Polish-Jewish coexistence—a factor which may seem so self-evident as not to bear noting—was that separateness and the failure to create a common sphere of interests and concerns. The cultural and spiritual gulf may have been breached by daily familiarity; but on the fundamental level, it was largely chosen on both sides. The barriers on the Polish side to full Jewish inclusion were high and well fortified; but the determination of most Jews to remain a "nation" apart from the surrounding majority was just as strong. I think that this sustained separateness led to what Zygmunt Bauman in his brilliant book *Modernity and the Holocaust* calls "the production of distance," and that it had a great bearing on what happened during the Holocaust. At the moment of greatest danger and vulnerability, it took qualities of exceptional moral strength and courage for a Polish person to help a Jewish one. In the eyes of most Poles, Jews were not within their natural sphere of responsibility; they were not, in the Polish expression, "ours."

What, then, can we in the "post-" generation do? What attitude should we take towards this painful history—and perhaps towards others? We are not in a position to demand justice, since the wrong was not done to us. And we are not in a position to forgive, since the wrong was not done to us. These are moral rights which belong to the participants in the events themselves; to assert or arrogate such rights for ourselves is, I think, an instance of false appropriation. A Truth and Reconciliation Commission is possible only in the immediate aftermath of horrific events. The privilege of demanding justice, and the magnanimity—I sometimes think the saintliness—of going beyond justice and choosing forgiveness over redress, belongs to those who have suffered. Any attempt to administer transgenerational justice is bound to get caught up in the cyclical logic of revenge—a logic evident, for example, in the recent wars in former Yugoslavia, in which the Serbs, with the help of a very long and stubborn collective memory, have been able to hearken back to their great defeat at the Battle of Kosovo in the fourteenth century as if it were a still present past, and could therefore view themselves as martyrs still at Muslim hands, and frame their campaigns of aggression as wars of redress.

These are some of the things we cannot do. But I think that the task in our generation is exactly to examine the past more strenuously, to press the questions raised by our memories—or, more frequently, received ideas—further; to lift, in other words, our own prohibitions on thought.

To return to the psychoanalytic model, it seems to me that, in our conceptualization of Holocaust memory, we are arrested in the early Freudian paradigm. That is, we talk of the return of repressed, traumatic memories, after a period of latency, of indifference and silence. There may be much truth in this; but, of course, as Freud came to understand, repressed memories never surface in their intact, mimetic state. Memory is never literal; it is precisely the faculty of selection, construction and reconstruction. Possibly for the subjects, the survivors themselves, there are certain memories that are so potent, or so unassimilable, that they continue to exist in the psyche in their unrevised state. But we, in the post-war generation, are not in that subject position; the memories that we speak about are not ours. We necessarily construct the past, and our task is to examine our own constructions. I realize that something in us balks at the notion of constructing, and thereby seemingly relativizing, the events of the Holocaust. Perhaps that is one reason why the formula of the unspeakable and the unimaginable—of the empty space of memory—seems fitting. But of course, even that formulation is itself a construction. The awful events may have been overwhelming to those who lived through them, but they were not, alas, unimaginable.

The psychoanalytic approach is highly suggestive for thinking about the processes of memory; but in addition it may be helpful in thinking about the relationship of the "post-" generation to its predecessors' experience. Psycho-analysis has taught us a lot about the impact of intimately transmitted trauma on its recipients—and for the literal second generation this is of utmost relevance. But it occurs to me that the "post-" generation as a whole is closer, in its relation-ship to the traumatic past, to the position of the analyst than the damaged analysand; and it strikes me that the model of the good analyst offers a fruitful paradigm for thinking about terrible histories which are close to us, but are not ours. In other words, I think that, from our position, it behooves us to think about the past with the utmost sympathy, or even empathy, for the participants, but at the same time, not to merge with the inner world of the participants entirely—and certainly, not to court such merging. It behooves us, with utmost compassion, to go beyond the point of trauma, as a good analyst would, to enable ourselves and perhaps even the victims themselves to process and think about what happened, and to understand the pre-traumatic history, so to speak, and the contexts of causes and meanings within which it took place.

The questions posed by the longer Polish-Jewish history certainly have important repercussions for Jewish self-conception; but, in addition, I think they have implications for the complex multicultural societies in which we live today. For a while, it has been necessary to foreground particular histories and memories, to articulate our differences. But it seems to me that we are at a moment when we need to reflect on how to combine the claims of distinct identities with those of social cohesion, how to create frameworks of common interest and concern which can encompass our separateness. And, if we are going to identify ourselves via our pasts, we need to have an apprehension of the fullness of those pasts—for no long history can assure any group of its instrinsic innocence, and no reading of a long history can sustain a notion of a totally alien Other.

In relation to the period of the Holocaust, and of World War II altogether, we are now at a crucial juncture, when living memory has to be relinquished. It is a poignant moment, akin to the moment of giving up mourning. In a sense, we need to make a choice as to whether in its relinquishment, the memory of the Holocaust will be passed on as myth or as history. I think there is much in the event that cries for transmutation into myth, which is the modality of deep emotion, and of awe. But I think we also have to follow the sterner gods of historical reflection and rigorous thought. If we do not, we run the risk of betraying the very legacy we are ostensibly honoring and preserving. We cannot undo the past, or even cure it. But we can derive from it an understanding that does justice to its richness and depth—and that can be potentially healing in its present and future uses.

Audience Comments

Audience Comment: What language did you do your interviews in?

Eva Hoffman: In Polish. I grew up in Poland, so I do speak Polish fluently. I did interviews both in Poland and with groups of survivors in the United States, mostly in Baltimore.

Audience Comment: Did you conduct any interviews in Yiddish?

Eva Hoffman: Well, fortunately everybody I spoke to did speak Polish, since I do not speak Yiddish.

Audience Comment: I was wondering if you could comment a bit about the state of memory current in Poland among non-Jews. How have they confronted the problem of memory and loss?

Eva Hoffman: There is a positive upsurge of reconsideration and thinking about memory. Poland's own communist decades, after all, were a period in which so much could not be spoken about publicly. There has also been a debate and discussion about the Polish relationship to the Jews and of Polish behavior towards the Jews during the war. The debate was often very rancorous but nevertheless very frank in catching every possible issue. And I do think in fact that it is very important to have voices from the Jewish inheritors of that history answer those debates.

Audience Comment: Since you alluded to the geographical distance of America, I wonder whether you ever come across questions raised by Americans and American Jews as to "Why didn't you European Jews manage to resist?", and if you do, what is your answer?

Eva Hoffman: That is perhaps the very nodal point of sensitivity. It seems to me that to an almost total extent resistance was impossible. I mean, once the Nazi intention of extermination and the whole mechanism of it was put in place, resistance was, well, if not entirely impossible, at least very difficult. At the same time, there are interesting studies just now being written and conducted which try to analyze why there wasn't more resistance. I mean there was of course the famous Hannah Arendt argument about the *Judenrat* but there are more interesting studies now which have to do with the state particularly of the shtetls before the war. With the enormous change and turmoil that the shtetl was undergoing right then, the old religious leadership which had been absolutely the uniform and unquestioned leadership for so many centuries all of a sudden had lost its authority, particularly over the young generation which was trying to enter the modern world. The conflict between generations was often very marked. So the old religious leadership was not in place and the new system of political life was still in enormous turbulence—the way of life was extremely fractured. There were fifteen political parties in Bransk, more parties throughout Poland. So there was no reservoir of coherent political leadership. And this is in fact an issue that does bear studying. I have heard survivors say that if there had been leadership they would have fought.

Audience Comment: You say there's a debate now about what happened during World War II. How about what's happening now? There are various stories about

Jews trying to move back to Poland. What is the current situation with anti-Semitism, would you say?

Eva Hoffman: I'm not sure that there are so many Jews trying to move back, although there are some. The current situation, once again, is very mixed. After 1989 there was a resurgence of anti-Semitic rhetoric even if it did not have any practical or functional repercussions. It was in fact a very strange rhetoric whereby people who were Catholic—Catholic leaders, for instance, the first post-1989 very devout Catholic president—were called "Jewish" if people did not like their liberalism or their democratic tendencies. There has been a resurgence of that. But there is also a resurgence of enormous interest in the Jewish Polish past.

In the town of Bransk, for example, I was being guided by a young man who didn't know anything about the town's Jewish history, but who started discovering traces of that history, such as gravestones, which were in various persons' homes or even embedded in the sidewalk. He became interested and is now a veritable archivist and is becoming a professional historian of that history. There are many people like that. There are Hebrew and Jewish and Yiddish courses given in various Polish schools. There is a kind of revival of Jewish life—Jewish communal life—within the post-war generation, which is very interesting. There's also what my Jewish friend in Poland, who's a kind of leader of the Jewish revival, calls "secondary anti-Semitism." In other words, the dialogue between Poles and Jews so far has been mutually very accusatory, mutually very defensive.

Audience Comment: I'd like to ask you a question about the two aspects of memory that you talked about. The first one, as I recall, is connected with survivors, a kind of Holocaust memory, the other being a "post-" memory. To me, that seems perfectly logical. But when you talk about the Holocaust you are talking about something almost outside of history. There's no agent in the idea of Holocaust—I mean the word itself is a kind of ritual offering—and it fits well with talking about survivors and their experience because you are dealing with something that they experienced internally and may not have a larger historical moment. But when you talk about "post-" history, you're already talking about a historical perspective on things and we expect that to be somewhat different. I'd like to call it "Nazi Genocide" or what have you, and put the agency right in it with the particulars of time. I was wondering what you think about that kind of division in thinking about that period.

Eva Hoffman: I'm not completely sure I understand the distinction you are drawing. I think there is certainly agency in the event which has come to be called the Holocaust, even if it is not in the etymology of the word itself. I'm not sure the nomenclature is so primary in this instance. We are talking about the event. I think there was agency and I think it was an agency of which the survivors were quite aware. Of course the experiences for the survivors were so overwhelming that for a long time it was very difficult to have a framework of understanding in which to place those experiences.

But what I'm saying about "post-" memory is that it often talks about memory as if memory itself somehow has agency, precisely as if the Holocaust is outside history—as if the Holocaust is memory itself. I don't know if that answers your question. This is one of the ambiguities or elisions in the study of Holocaust memory. What I'm advocating really is a "post-" memory which will give an interpretive framework to it.

Audience Comment: I do think that the word makes a great deal of difference. I saw a tape of an oral history done at Yale or someplace. The woman first talked about her childhood, about how it was wonderful in the shtetl, and then she said that when she was in the camp, she was watching the trains coming in and a whole wedding party arrived and then she said they went up in smoke, in flames, as if no one had done it, and it made no difference who did it, the experience itself was the difference. I can understand "Holocaust" being used that way. But when you deal with "post-" memory—and that's what I liked about your distinction—it tries to recreate at least in that space a separate or historical perspective, a perspective in which you try to bring together a lot of information.

Eva Hoffman: The word "Holocaust," of course, didn't come into use until considerably later.

Audience Comment: I guess the message is that this is a complex subject and I think we are beginning to appreciate that deeply. [applause]

Audience Comment: Being Polish but not Jewish, I'd like to express my admiration for an extremely balanced assessment of all this very difficult, very complex Polish-Jewish history. And, again, this is only my personal assessment, but if someone in Poland were to hear your lecture today, this grotesque anti-Semitism that we experience in Poland today would probably not exist. Your talk touched me very much. Thank you. [applause]

Born in Poland in 1945, writer EVA HOFFMAN is the author of several books, including the widely regarded *Lost in Translation: A Life in a New Language* and most recently *Shtetl: The Life and Death of a Small Town and the World of Polish Jews*. Having received a Ph.D. in English and American Literature from Harvard, Hoffman has taught literature and creative writing at several institutions including Columbia University, the University of Minnesota, and Tufts; she was an editor and writer at the *New York Times* from 1979-1990, serving as senior editor of "The Book Review" from 1987-1990.